99 THOUGHTS FOR YOUTH WORKERS

99 Thoughts for Youth Workers
Random Insightful Tips for Anyone in Youth Ministry

Copyright © 2009 Josh Griffin
Visit our website: **simplyyouthministry.com**

Credits
Author: Josh Griffin
Executive Developer: Nadim Najm
Chief Creative Officer: Joani Schultz
Assistant Editor: Rob Cunningham
Cover Art Director: Jeff Storm
Designer: Veronica Lucas
Production Manager: DeAnne Lear

Unless otherwise indicated, all Scripture quotations are taken from the Holy Bible, New Living Translation, copyright © 1996, 2004. Used by permission of Tyndale House Publishers, Inc., Carol Stream, Illinois 60188. All rights reserved.

Library of Congress Cataloging-in-Publication Data

Griffin, Joshua, 1974-
99 thoughts for youth workers : random insightful tips for anyone in youth ministry / by Joshua Griffin. —1st American pbk. p. cm. Includes bibliographical references and index. ISBN 978-0-7644-6301-3 (pbk. : alk. paper) 1. Church work with youth. I. Title. II. Title: Ninety-nine thoughts for youth workers. BV4447.G68 2009 259'.23—dc22   2009023014

10 9   17 16 15
Printed in the United States of America.

Over the past couple of years, I've been journaling my thoughts about youth ministry. When I had a learning, I wrote it down in my Moleskine™ or posted it on my blog.

This is a collection of those thoughts.

If you want to read more in real time, join the youth ministry conversation at **www.morethandodgeball.com**. I post there every single day and would love to have you join me in the journey.

Just so you know, I quit youth ministry every Sunday night and sign up again every Tuesday morning. My prayer is that these somewhat random and potentially insightful thoughts about our profession encourage you in what I feel is the greatest calling of all – youth ministry.

Joshua Griffin
High School Pastor
Saddleback Church

TABLE OF CONTENTS

OKAY...SO THERE ARE ACTUALLY 113 THOUGHTS IN THIS BOOK. SORRY I COULDN'T STICK TO 99 —BUT IF YOU LIKE FREE STUFF AS MUCH AS I DO. YOU'LL ENJOY A FEW EXTRA.

{ Thoughts 01-36 }

4 YOUTH MINISTRY INSTINCTS

There are things you have to do instinctively as a youth worker. I like to think of these as our default settings, the "automatics" when there's no other direction. When you're wondering what to do — this is what to do. These four things have to be second nature:

01 GOD: CHECK MY HEART

Youth ministry can be intensely demanding, and nothing less than a completely dependent relationship with God will do.

- Am I walking close to the Father?
- Is this a job or a ministry?
- What is my attitude telling others right now?

02 ME: TAKE INITIATIVE

Youth ministry needs people of action. If you're always waiting to be told what to do, you're holding the team back. Jump in and take something to the next level, or brainstorm about what might be — then start running to take the team there.

- Where can I be of help?
- What needs to be done right now?
- Is there something new I can do to help us fulfill our purposes?

03 VOLUNTEERS: BRING SOMEONE ALONG

Youth ministry isn't meant to be done alone. Any project you are working on should have some volunteer component. Many hands make the load light.

- Is there an adult volunteer I can share this with?
- Who on our volunteer team could take charge of this?
- Is there a student leader who has the skill for this project?

04 STUDENTS: PUT THE "CUSTOMER" FIRST

Youth ministry needs "people" people. We cannot ignore needs in order to get tasks done.

- Am I balancing people and tasks?
- Is there somebody I need to serve right now?
- Did I return those phone calls this week?
- What conversation am I avoiding?

3 WAYS YOUTH MINISTRY CAN SUPPORT THE CHURCH

Youth ministry is not an island unto itself. The tail cannot wag the dog. It is not a separate ministry of the church, doing its own thing with its own agenda. Youth ministry is a part of the greater whole. Once we see ourselves as a part of what God is doing throughout the congregation, we will serve the church better. Here are some basic principles to help your church win through your youth ministry becoming a vibrant part of the whole, not just a drain on the resources and facilities.

05 CLEAN UP AFTER YOURSELF

Simple rule: Leave it better than how you found it. Clean out the church van – and if you really want to shock a trustee, wash it and fill it up after your youth activity. It might give someone a heart attack, which in many churches is the only way to get "stuck" leadership to move on. Just assume your youth room is going to be used by everyone, so make sure it is clean and ready to go for someone else after your service. There's nothing worse than having a great spiritual high sucked out of you when you get caught leaving the place looking like a dump.

06 PLAN AN EVENT THAT SUPPORTS THE CHURCH

Find a way to support other parts of the church – don't always be inward-focused. How can you support the mission efforts of the church? Can you serve the children's ministry? This year we hosted a special Halloween party for the children of our church organized by students in our high school small groups. Our children's ministry didn't need our help, but we wanted to support the church and provide opportunities for our students to serve.

07 BE THE FIRST TO BE FLEXIBLE

Youth ministry often sits at the bottom of the totem pole (on the church website your picture is just under the janitor's volunteer part-time assistant, right?), so let's embrace it! Your space isn't sacred – learn that early or pay the price later. If something trumps the activity you had planned, fight to find a way to make it work rather than fight the people moving in on your territory.

There are certainly hills you should die on, but be flexible and maintain a whole-church heart. That way, you die for something worth fighting for.

3 WAYS TO GET CHIPS IN YOUR POCKET

In some ways, we should always go back to basics and the fundamentals of youth ministry, no matter where we are in the youth ministry journey. Here are three ways to get some chips in your youth ministry credibility bank right from the start – if you ever have to push "all in," these will come in handy:

08 COMMUNICATE... NO. OVER-COMMUNICATE

I'm confident that no parent in church history has ever said to a youth worker, "I just wish our youth ministry would communicate less with our family." Instead, I'm always wondering if we communicate frequently and effectively enough. Are we really expecting that a promo flyer handed to a student will make it home? When was our website last updated? Have we clearly articulated the vision for the change, or are we expecting word to just somehow get out? List all of the ways you're communicating – then ask, "Is my message really getting out?"

09 SHOW UP DURING A CRISIS

Youth ministry shines when pastors and volunteers step up during a crisis. The opposite is almost always true – youth ministry takes a huge hit when someone's urgency doesn't elicit a matching urgent response. It only takes a few days of "not getting to it" before irreparable trust damage is done. Knowing when to drop everything to help a family in need will become a huge win for your youth ministry future. Reflect for just a second on whom you should call or visit before you leave the office today.

10 MAKE MEETINGS WORTH IT

If you're going to ask people to meet with you, make it worth their time. In just a few minutes your volunteers know if you've really planned the time together or if you're making it up as you go. Parents are eager to see an inside glimpse at what the youth ministry is doing, but the enthusiasm can quickly be doused if you're unprepared. If you're leading the meeting, start on time, end early, and make everything in-between remarkable – or else people may pray for you to have a heart attack so something interesting happens. And ask for their input – you'll get a ton of feedback, and people will feel valued because they were heard. So look over the agenda for your next meeting – if it can be emailed with minimal instruction, do that and save the meeting time for significance.

5 WAYS TO BE A BETTER MANAGER

I've been thinking about what a manager must do to be successful. Here's a few of my recent learnings on the subject:

11 DON'T JUST BE A LAUNCHER

There's nothing worse than a person who fires and forgets. A good manager is a launcher and a sustainer. Personality excuses aside, a good manager will walk alongside a ministry team even when the "shiny and new" has run off of it. Launch, sustain, and evaluate.

12 **TALK** TO PEOPLE, NOT ABOUT PEOPLE

If someone drops the ball, everyone has the tendency to talk about that person, without talking to that person. There's nothing more destructive than when the team leader talks about someone behind his or her back, or allows other members of the team to do the same. When someone talks poorly about someone else, I try to say, "Have you talked to that person about it?" Imagine a team that worked this way, instead of sabotaging the efforts from the inside out.

Youth Ministry is a Calling of Extremes

Youth ministry is a calling of extremes. This week not a single day was the same as the last. I've ministered on both ends of the extremes — students who are taking huge God steps forward and students who are making the worst choices possible and completely headed downhill. Youth ministry pays extreme — extremely little! Youth ministry is about asking a student to give over total control of his or her life to Jesus — an absolute extreme. We minister under extreme pressure from senior pastors, staff, parents — and if you're like me — from yourself.

Extreme hours, extreme emotions, extreme work. So why would anyone want to do it? Seems like a nice, safe, well-paying nine-to-five job is more what people look for in life. Extreme fulfillment. Glad we're in it together, friend.

13 BE WISE IN "THINKING OUT LOUD"

Verbal processing kills camaraderie. A leader of an organization can rarely share inside information with the team without creating an exclusive group of insiders. Unless you want to quickly alienate and create silos of misinformation and mistrust, be careful not to say too much out loud before you land on a decision.

14 PREPARE PEOPLE FOR AN ANNOUNCEMENT

If you're about to drop a bomb or change the direction of your student ministry, it shouldn't be a surprise to the people it affects the most. Have a few conversations prior to announcing the decision, to prepare people for sweeping change.

15 TALK ABOUT WHAT IS OBVIOUSLY BEING AVOIDED

The elephant in the room is when everyone knows about the conflict, but no one ever takes steps to resolve it. There's tension, but no one will make that first move toward reconciliation. Remove your team's questions and the uncertainty of leadership by bringing up the ugly stuff, knowing that journeying through it together will make you stronger.

16 CONNECT WITH GOD

Sadly, it seems the easiest thing to let slip on a daily basis is my own spiritual growth. Quickly moving from a total dependence on God to naïve reliance on my own gifts and abilities certainly equals disaster. You can carry the weight of the world for a few steps, but then it will come crashing down on you. Warning: If you haven't committed your day and your way to God today, you're asking for shock wave-causing burnout.

17 CONNECT WITH A VOLUNTEER

Every single day I want to interact with a volunteer. Maybe it is just a text message, maybe a quick email. Maybe it's coffee or my favorite… lunch. If a day goes by when I'm not connecting with a volunteer, I'm wasting my shepherding time and jeopardizing the infrastructure for growth in our student ministry.

18 CONNECT WITH YOUR PHILOSOPHY

Somewhere over time we drift. We drift from volunteers, we drift from God, and we drift from the core values and philosophy we know we should be following. Recently I reread Doug Fields' *Purpose-Driven Youth Ministry* just to make sure I was in touch with the direction I felt our ministry should be headed. Connecting with your philosophy will help you continue to cast vision to your leadership, and it will make you contagious to your team.

19 CONNECT WITH THE TEAM

Speaking of team, that's one place a little energy should be focused every day as well. Whether it is with a trustee over the vans or a deacon about an upcoming baptism, spend some time investing relationally. Shoot a note to your senior pastor, talk about transition with the volunteer college director, or find someone on the team to push toward unity. Talk about success and failures. You just might learn something and encourage everyone to work better together!

20 CONNECT WITH FAMILY

Margin is always out of whack for most youth workers. I'm raising my hand high on this one. I was running on empty this past week, coming off of a great weekend and a ton of work for a youth ministry conference, then heading straight into another weekend. I'm actually looking forward to a break because things will slow down. I spent half of yesterday and today resting, playing video games, laughing with the kids, and running errands with the family. We caught a movie, grabbed some Chick-fil-A® and hey, I might even get to bed early tonight. Refuse to cave in on family time.

21 CONNECT WITH A STUDENT

It would be a mistake to not connect with a student every day. Shoot a text message of encouragement to a student (or a few at once, they probably won't know) or take the time to jot a handwritten note to a student who could use it. I like that one a lot because parents usually pick up the snail mail, and they a) can read the full text of the postcard, too or b) know that an envelope addressed to their son/daughter from the church is a big deal.

22 CONNECT WITH A PARENT

It would be a good move to connect with a parent every day. Unfortunately, we typically only connect with them when they've screwed up, we've screwed up, or their child has screwed up. How big of a deal would it be for you to let them know you're praying for them? I think it could make a huge difference, but few of us will ever know because we haven't traveled very far down this road.

23 CONNECT WITH THE CALENDAR

What needs to be marketed? What should be added? Do the events on the calendar match up with our philosophy? Is there adequate "margin" in the calendar? What could be handed off, what could be delegated? Let the calendar speak to other areas of your ministry; it will usually do a lot of talking.

24 CONNECT WITH RESOURCES

Coming up with material each week is next to impossible, so take some time to Google the topic you're looking for or spend time on trusted youth ministry resource websites to aid you in your ministry. You don't have to reinvent the wheel every weekend. I'm sure some of the most effective resources are made by a local youth worker, but at the same time there's plenty out there to at least help you get off to a good start.

25 CONNECT WITH FUN

Take a break! Watch *The Office*. Laugh out loud today. Bookmark Dave Barry's blog. Laugh with your kids — maybe play a silly game at dinner. Do something stupid. Get a tattoo (I'm joking … or just make sure there's a cross or a Jesus-fish in it somewhere). Let your hair down; it might be just the thing you need to get over the hurdle in sermon preparation or help you relax after dealing with a difficult situation. But hey — just be sure you don't Twitter™ away your life.

I got to spend some quality time with my team at a youth ministry conference. The more memories we share, the more experiences we collect, the more inside jokes we create, and the more laughs we enjoy — the more we bond as a team. Here are four more ways you can be a better teammate starting today:

26 ASK HOW YOU CAN PITCH IN

The lost art of teamwork calls for you to peek your head out of your office every once in a while. If all you do is work in your specialty with your head down, you miss the chance to take your team beyond the expected. Maybe take a few minutes to think about how you can help your church pull off the adult retreat and children's event, too. If you take a 30-minute break from student tasks, it could create a serious amount of goodwill within the church culture and possibly give you people to rely on when you're in a pinch, too.

27 BRING SOMETHING TO THE MEETING

If you're headed into a meeting, be a good teammate and be prepared for it. Spend a few minutes in research. Spend a few minutes coming up with ideas. Spend a few minutes praying about it. Spend a few minutes searching for a solution to the problem you're meeting about. The meeting doesn't start when everyone gets there; be prepared before you walk through the door.

28 FIND THE POSITIVE

What energy are you bringing to the day? Today, I know I have to start out on a tough note -- address an area of conflict with someone. But I can't let that create a negative outlook for my team or our future. Focus on the positive things you specifically notice, and be an encourager.

29 BALANCE WORK AND PLAY

You need to be a teammate that gets stuff done and can be counted on, but don't be afraid to play a little bit, too. Take a minute to watch that YouTube™ video, grab a coffee with someone, or talk about that crazy thing someone did on their day off. Too often we jump right into work and keep working straight through the week. The best teams love each other enough to talk about non-work life, pop culture, and experiences. Goof-off one afternoon. Go see a movie together. Whatever it takes, make sure there's an element of fun in whatever you do. The team that plays together, stays together.

4 INPUTS I'M REDUCING

A good leader has many inputs to help develop strong output, but right now it is time for me to focus on fewer inputs to reduce the noise. Here's what I'm doing in the digital world to make sure I'm hearing what is important and not just filtering through piles and piles of stuff to find the good stuff.

30 BEING SELECTIVE WITH THE BLOGS I READ

I'm reducing the number of blogs I read because some of the sources aren't contributing to my journey. Not all blogs are worth reading, so I'm removing the feeds I used to like, blogs that have really dropped in quality content, or blogs I bookmarked on a whim in the first place. Blogs that are only a distraction aren't worth following, but some of them may still be worth visiting from time to time.

31 REDUCING THE NUMBER OF TWITTERERS I FOLLOW

I love Twitter™, but there's a ton of noise coming through that channel as well. I dropped about 40% of the people I was following, not because I don't like them but because everything was getting too noisy and it was time to cut it out.

32 REMOVING INSTANT MESSENGER

This morning I deleted my chat program. Honestly, I didn't use this input that much, so it was the easiest to let go. It set up false expectations that I could be reached every time I sat down at the computer and was just a general bother. Gone!

33 DELETING MY MYSPACE™ ACCOUNT

This one was long overdue, as I have become the worst MySpacer ever, logging in once a month at best. It was hard to give up my big-time status with 622 friends (ha!), but let's be honest – Facebook™ is a better tool right now and this one is just leftover noise.

Are you reducing any noise in your life this week?
Do it!

SLEEP IS NOT A SIGN OF WEAKNESS

I posted a poll on my blog to get a little background on the sleep habits of youth workers. I wasn't surprised to see that only 21% of youth workers who responded got eight or more hours of sleep on a typical night. What's the deal?

For some reason, people who sleep more seem to get a bad rep – suggesting that the need for sleep somehow makes you weak. And while I seem to be able to get by with a little less sleep than normal (I average 6-7 hours a night), there are some great benefits to a youth worker getting some serious rest. Here are a few reasons you should skip late-night television and sleep in late "accidentally" once a month:

34 SLEEP GIVES YOU A CHANCE TO CLEAR YOUR HEAD FOR DECISIONS

Make that big decision in the morning! If there's any way possible to make a call the next day instead of under pressure when you're fried at the end of the day, move it to the morning. A good night's rest often has a clearing effect – plan your most important meetings first thing.

35 SLEEP GIVES YOU A CHANCE TO COOL OFF FROM CONFLICT

If there's tension in a relationship or an urge to respond to an email that triggers you, save it as a draft and wait until morning. You'll be more likely to respond in a Christ-like way after a good night's rest. Rarely will you regret a slightly delayed decision; too often the next morning you'll regret the decision made the night before. Don't respond and regret. There's a reason the phrase "sleep on it" has survived even in our fast-paced society.

36 SLEEP ENCOURAGES BALANCE IN YOUR LIFE

We need rest. We can't escape it! Try as we might, a lack of sleep will eventually catch up with us. Focus on balance in your schedule with adequate time for tasks, relationships, and rest.

Take 15 minutes right now and turn off the Outlook™ inbox alert and Twitter™ chatter in the background. Spend some time in the dark and rest for a few moments. Maybe you should just close this book and go to sleep! See you in the morning.

4 ASSUMPTIONS DURING THE BUSY SEASON

We've just finished the summer of what we've called "tree lot" season, the temporary but extremely busy season of ministry when you have to get the trees out the door before Christmas arrives. As that is coming to an end, we're really gearing up for another season of the same: fast-paced, high-expectation ministry. In essence, we just got another shipment of trees to last us until Christmas and it is time to go at it again.

Here are four assumptions I asked our teams to make during the next few months of ministry:

37 ASSUME GOD IS GOING TO WORK THROUGH YOUR WORK

Too often we concentrate on the "work" part of the busy season, staying late and growing frustrated when we bump shoulders with the same people more often than normal. It is too easy to forget that God is going to use us – that each conversation, each time we connect with another volunteer, each line of the infinitely-complex spreadsheet is part of us contributing to what God is doing. Yes, we have to work hard. Yes, we should expect to work late. But God is up to something – His Spirit is at work in our work.

38 ASSUME THAT PERSON NEEDS HELP WITH A PROJECT

This is the team mindset that we all need when the pace increases. Just assume that someone needs help – besides, work is a lot more fun in pairs than alone. Clear your plate and pitch in – they'll do the same when you need it, too.

39 ASSUME THE NEXT PERSON YOU SEE NEEDS ENCOURAGEMENT

If I'm honest, I would say that our culture is thirsty for this. I think our humor-heavy, dry sense of sarcasm is welcome (it can even be a form of encouragement), but there's nothing wrong with a "good job" or lifting up someone's arm as the winner after a long fight. Assume that person hasn't been thanked or celebrated in a while.

40 ASSUME THAT YOU ARE THE RIGHT PERSON TO DO YOUR JOB

This is where you trust the leadership of the church and God's Spirit at work. God has called you to work with students. God didn't mistakenly put you in the position you hold – He created it for you in this moment. In the busyness of the now-extended tree lot season, let's not forget our shared passion for our students and this thing we call youth ministry.

EVERYTHING IS THE MESSAGE

I want students to walk away from the weekend worship service (our entry-level program) with the big idea. I want them to "get" the sermon in a sentence – stuck in their heads with creativity, skill, and passion. I want visual learners to get it, note-takers to get it, freshmen through seniors to get it; I want the uninterested to be drawn in and the regulars engaged week after week.

With that in mind, I've felt more and more lately that the sermon, while perhaps king of the weekend, is only a part of the message. Essentially, I'm saying that "the message" isn't the only message. Here are some thoughts on the breakdown of the weekend in terms of the message:

41 THE SERMON/TALK

Definitely 40-50% of the overall message rests on the speaker. In our current format, the speaker is the most focused part of the night on the series subject. He or she takes God's Word and applies it directly and formally to the lives of high school students. Knowing that significance, series topics and speaker choice are a very big deal.

42 THE MUSIC/WORSHIP

A strong 20-30% of the night's message falls into this category. The songs that are picked, the lyrics of songs, prayer, other elements of worship – they all should point toward the message. The right songs and the right tempo of music are crucial to the overall message of the night. Singing "God of Wonders" or "Let Me Sing" during our *Save the Planet* series reinforced the importance of that part of the message.

43 THE ATMOSPHERE

10-15% of the message falls on the atmosphere. Did we create an atmosphere that leads people to the message? Are the banners, signage, and a bulletin all consistent with the message? Does the weekend look thrown together, or does it look planned out and prepared? Is there an air of excellence – are we treating the topic of the night with with the respect it deserves? A good atmosphere sets up a a great speaker. The opposite is also true.

44 THE PROGRAMMING

In my mind, programming carries 15-20% of that nights message. The clip from *Wall-E* during the opening of the night sets the tone for caring for creation. The cinderblock we smashed as an example of the way we treat the earth will be remembered for a long time. The program is a great way to make things stick.

I understand the importance of the message. I understand God chose preachers and they should… well, preach. But I also understand that the message is way, way bigger than a 30-minute talk.

What a great weekend service – thank You, God! Now, okay if I take Monday off … I have just five days to do it allover again. Sigh.

I don't know a single youth pastor who hasn't felt like this. In fact, it's Tuesday morning and I feel this way right now. I actually took a day off this week. My daughter's birthday is tonight, and I'm spending some quality time with my family Wednesday afternoon. Which is all fine and dandy, but the weekend service is the Cloverfield beast that just can't be brought down. It doesn't sneak up on you; it is anindestructible monster that terrorizes youth workers night and day.

We try to spend significant time each week debriefing our programs. It's not just so we can continually get better. It's also because we'll never find a good place of balance in our personal lives if we don't come up for a breath of air sometimes. Youth ministry happens at light speed, and it is critical you spend a few minutes debriefing what was great, what was unnecessary, and how to find the appropriate balance between "the grind" and your family.

With that in mind, here are the four big-picture questions we try to ask after each outing. Most are based on some basic principles in chapter seven of Doug Fields' book, *Purpose-Driven Youth Ministry*.

45 INVOLVEMENT

How did we use volunteers this week?
Students and volunteers both are included in this simple question. How did we utilize students in the weekend experience? Were there students on stage? Were there an

adequate number of student greeters? Did the volunteers feel part of the weekend process, or did they feel like spectators? Did all our volunteers feel like their service was appreciated? Did we work together as a team?

46 ENVIRONMENT

Did we center on community/crowd students? Could a "first-time" student easily navigate the experience? There's enough confusion and anxiety in just showing up! Did we use insider language that alienates outsiders? Was our topic something a typical student could connect with?

47 ENGAGEMENT

Was the night fun and the message understandable? Was there an element of fun? Did you see students smiling? Could students relate to the teacher and the teaching? Was the message relevant to their lives? Did we have a takeaway or action step that is applicable to their lives?

48 IMPROVEMENT

What ways could we specifically improve next week? What do we have to change? What do we need to take a risk on and try? What has to change next week to make sure we are the most effective we can be? Do we need to change course, or are we on target?

Let's kill the weekend beast! Spend some time debriefing the weekend so you can be better prepared and more effective, and set the stage for God to do something great in the lives of students.

1, 5, 7, 10

7 SIGNS YOU MIGHT COUNT LIKE A SENIOR PASTOR

Numbers do not equal results. But like it or lump it, the headcount at your youth program matters to your church.

And the problem with this is that youth pastors count terribly — it is a proven fact. I think it might even be a recessive gene found universally in pastors! When faced with any size crowd, a pastor quickly assesses the room with a margin of error of plus or minus about 150. Actually, I've never met a pastor who counted minus, so it would be plus 150. Either way, here are seven ways to know if you count like a senior pastor:

49

You count band members, student leaders, staff, and volunteers each of your multiple services.

50

You count empty seats instead of filled ones, and subtract that number from the room's fire capacity.

51

You don't even bother to count; you close your eyes and optimistically ask God to speak to you the grand total. Or you use the Force.

52

If someone enters the room for a few minutes then leaves, you still add that person to your count. If it is the senior pastor/elder/deacon, you are in such shock and awe that you forget your count and you have to start all over again. You immediately mentally begin to prepare statements defending the attendance.

53

If a pregnant woman or someone enters carrying an infant, they totally count as two. You secretly pray for triplets inside the womb of an expectant mother on your volunteer team.

54

You vigorously disagree with the actual count when someone else does the counting. There's no way it could possibly have been that low – the room was packed!

55

If a student goes to the bathroom and comes back, bingo! Add them in again without thinking twice.

This Makes It All Worth While

I haven't taken a shower in 5 days. To get to our destination on this mission trip, I've driven 15 hours in a RV across 3 states. I can now say I've survived a carnival in a sandstorm. It's only a matter of time before I'm "dunk tanked" late tonight by a laughing mob after chapel. I can now officially say I've eaten dust-flavored cotton candy. I moderately injured a student by driving over some huge speedbumps just a little too fast. I'm scared to death of all of the street dogs around our base camp. I still haven't had a Navajo taco.

And I can't stop smiling from ear to ear.

Max was forced to come on this trip. He got caught tagging and his parents said he could be grounded for 3 months or go on this 1-week trip with our high school ministry. Can you guess which one chose? The lesser of the two punishments — going on a church event for a few days. Gotta love that. But here's the deal — in the craziness of this week — work projects, dusty carnivals, dunk tanks and long distance driving — God showed up. He reached into this kid's heart and he accepted Christ. He has never been to our church, never been into a service, never even prayed before. His first prayer to God was giving Him his life.

There are a lot of days that make me question my calling. The church politics I've briefly escaped from during this trip will return in 48 hours. All of the stuff we put up with to do youth ministry is still present... but days like this make it all worthwhile.

There are many elements of healthy communication during the weekend service. These are not exclusive; in my mind each of these weaves together to cast a compelling message. These are not about personal style, but tools to connect the audience to the message:

56 HUMOR

One of the universal languages of humanity is laughter. Laughter breaks down barriers and disarms people to accept truth. The highs of laughter make the serious points that much more compelling. I love listening to people who can make me laugh but cram truth down my throat at the same time. Use humor in some form every week – you don't have to be funny to have fun.

57 CALL TO ACTION

A great way to connect with your audience is to call them to something much bigger than they dreamed possible. Show them what could be, and take them places they didn't know about. Dare to challenge students to live a different life with a practical action step connected to the weekend.

58 AUTHENTICITY

Find ways to inject yourself into your talk to demonstrate the journey of following Christ. Unpack your life with your learnings, struggles, and flaws. Show that you are human and not always the hero.

59 OBJECT LESSONS

Several of my favorite moments of the "talk" haven't been the talk at all. Illustrations or object lessons can help connect students to a particular concept more easily. Recently, we talked about the debt we owe Christ by dropping $100 in nickels on the floor – a compelling image of forgiveness of our debt through Jesus. Before that we used a little water dropper to show the world's love, and a pitcher to show God's overflowing love for us – and a challenge to settle for nothing less. Use images like this to memorably connect.

60 USING MULTIPLE SENSES

Don't let students just hear you for half an hour. If you're talking about an upcoming mission trip, have sample food from the country where you'll be ministering. If the story is about Jesus in the desert, turn up the heat in the room. Okay, don't be lame, but think about ways to connect more than the ears to the message.

61 TESTIMONY

Students will pay near-perfect attention when another student is speaking on stage. Not too long ago we had a super powerful testimony of an 18-year-old atheist who is now a Christ-follower. Use a testimony to show a next step and/or the benefit of choosing the way God asks us to live—I bet it will totally connect.

These four points about dealing with student testimonies in a service might be helpful. We've recently added to these guidelines after some challenges with student stories on stage. So powerful, but they really have to be done right. They are worth all of the work!

62 WRITE IT OUT

No student should get up on stage without having the testimony prepared in advance. There's nothing more powerful than a student story to complement the message, but it can become awkward or even distracting when a student doesn't have a clear focus and a well-written script. Write it down and have the student read it for the delivery. It evens the playing field so average students sound just like the ones that are more comfortable on stage.

63 EDIT IT DOWN

Typically the testimony doesn't come in at just the right size, and your size might fluctuate based on the needs of the service or the strength of the story. Either way, edit it down to perfectly fit the theme and message. Remove all last names, check the facts, remove sentences that might appear to approve of unbecoming behavior, and make sure to edit out extra details that color the story but may distract.

64 TALK TO PARENTS

Before a student hits the stage, make sure his/her parents (if applicable) are in the loop. There's nothing worse than a parent being blindsided – make sure there are no surprises. The story needs to be filtered by the family, and make sure they are prepared for consequences and/or repercussions from the testimony.

65 THANK THE STUDENT

It is a huge thing for students to share their story! A handwritten card is a big deal; perhaps a small gift or a follow-up coffee is in order. Thank the student for participating in a service where life change is the goal, and be sure to share the results of the weekend.

THANKS!

SMALL GROUPS AND EVENTS

{ Thoughts 66-86 }

4 PLACES TO RECRUIT VOLUNTEERS

There are a bunch of sources for potential volunteers — I thought I would list four of my favorites to help spur you on to a successful youth ministry filled with volunteers. We're always working on this one, too!

66 ADULT SERVICES

When was the last time you were on the adult service stage recruiting volunteers? While this one is obvious, sometimes the obvious is ignored. Bulletin insert? Promo video? Take some time and create something special so that when you do get stage time, you make it count.

67 PARENT MEETINGS

Youth workers often shy away from parents as volunteers, but in all honesty, there are some great youth worker parents out there. I do think you have to find the right person, so don't take just anyone and be especially leery of the ones that are a little too eager to get involved.

68 CONFERENCES, SPECIAL MEETINGS, RETREATS

There's often a moment at the end of a conference or retreat where people make a commitment. They take a step toward growth and accept a challenge. I want our student ministry to be right there with an HSM (High School Ministry) card in hand ready for that conversation. Check the church calendar or website and look for these types of opportunities.

69 COLLEGE MINISTRY

Why not drop into your college ministry next week and see if you can round up some new small group leaders? Don't expect a one-time recruitment to be successful; you might have to develop a relationship of trust to gather up some great students. And remember this will be hit and miss; college students have tough schedules and can get flaky. But the star volunteers you discover will be worth it.

I made some promises to our small group leaders during our small group training. These quotes aren't quite verbatim, but here's the gist of what I said we would do. We have a lot to live up to in these simple statements:

70 "WE WILL RESPOND TO YOU NO LATER THAN THE NEXT DAY."

We will be available to you when you need us the most — within 24 hours of your contact. If you send us an email with a request for prayer, we will pray for you. If you need a resource, we'll find it, and if possible get it in your hands. If you're having trouble with a student, we'll help in whatever way you need. If you have a tough situation and don't know what to do, we'll go over some responses and help coach you to the desired result. Anything less than a near-immediate, caring, and active response is unacceptable. Unless I've communicated that I'm taking some time away, you can count on me. Availability.

71 "YOU WILL BE TREATED LIKE FAMILY."

We will eat together around a table once a week. We will pray together. We will share hurts, ideas, love, celebrations, problems, and praises. We will know each other's names and smile when we see each other around the church. We will take a genuine interest in family, life, job, and calling. If there is tension, we'll step aside and address it and present a unified front to students. We will not accept lone rangers and rogues — we are going to be a great team. Family.

Youth Ministry Seasons of Experience

How long have you been in youth ministry? I recently celebrated thirteen in the game but remember my rookie season like it was yesterday. I made every mistake humanly possible. It is only by God's grace that I'm still in youth ministry.

Youth ministry years of experience should be measured a little differently. I think they're more like taking the pounding of a football season. You love it, you're called to it, but they aren't easy on the body. The next time you reflect on your years in youth ministry, maybe think seasons of experience.

In your first year, you're a rookie. No shame in that, everyone has to get his or her start.

In your first few years, you've got a couple of seasons under your belt. You've got some experience, and you're sticking around the big leagues.

If you've been in youth ministry for 5ish years, you're a veteran with great leadership on your team. You might get nominated for a Pro-Bowl appearance.

If you've stuck it out in youth ministry for 10 or more years, you've taken big hits and lived to talk about it. You've been knocked down a few times, but you keep getting back up. In some ways, you're a shoe-in Hall of Famer.

I don't know what season of youth ministry you are in, but I'm glad you're on the team.

We laid out our High School Ministry calendar this past week – it was a great time of focusing our energy on the direction of our ministry. The process we followed to get our calendar set up went really well, so I thought it might be helpful as you work ahead, too:

72 STRIVE FOR BALANCE

The first mission is for the leadership to be clear that one purpose or agenda isn't going to dominate our calendar. We are a youth ministry that wants to be driven by the biblical purposes of the Great Commandment and the Great Commission. We will spend time talking about evangelism, fellowship, discipleship, ministry, and worship – but not letting any one thing drive the direction.

73 TAKE ONE PURPOSE AND RUN WITH IT

After the balance conversation, we spend time going through each month, putting on events, classes, trips, and meetings that focus on one purpose. We also look at what we did the previous year and debrief them on the fly. If they worked, we consider them for the new year. If they didn't, we do our best to go after something fresh. So we look at the beginning and talk just discipleship, then move on, focusing on that one purpose.

74 REPEAT THAT PROCESS FOR THE FIVE PURPOSES

Then we go month by month again, this time through the eyes of evangelism. After that we hit fellowship dates for small groups, and then drop in discipleship retreats, camps, and trainings. The goal is for each purpose to be represented clearly on the calendar.

75 DROP IN THE DEADLINES

Once the calendar is more or less "set" we drop in deadlines for registrations and various milestones related to the projects. For example, our mission trip requires a registration start and end, as well as three parent meetings and a celebration weekend. Small groups don't just start on day one; they need registration dates, deadlines, and enough time for us to process the students into groups. When you plan an event, be sure to also include the follow-up dates as well.

76 LOOK AT THE BIG PICTURE AND CUT AWAY

Then we look at the overall big picture and goal for balance and health and start the painful process of figuring out what needs to be cut. We look for ways to consolidate events when possible, to reduce the number of nights students and volunteers are out.

8 IMPERATIVES FOR THE BIG EVENT PLANNING MEETING

This is it — the big meeting. You sit down in a room with your volunteers. Some are long-term veterans, some are newbies. There might be a few student leaders, maybe an intern, or even a few others on your paid team. There's some early banter among friends, a few introductions, then all eyes turn to you — the fearless leader of the big event.

You can feel it in your gut. This is the start of the countdown. This is the first, defining moment that signals the planned launch of the unbelievably exciting, maybe even uncomfortably large, task God has placed on your heart. You know that what you say now will define how the next couple months play out. What are the basic things your team needs to know? How do you mix inspiration with specific direction?

You take a deep breath and then start talking.

77 HEART/HISTORY: TELL THE STORY OF WHY

Why are we doing this event? Why is it critical that we all show up for this thing? Why are your volunteers taking time off to be at this event? This is your chance to really "sell" the event to the leadership, and it should flow out of a passionate heart for God and students.

78 TARGET AUDIENCE/PURPOSE: WHOM ARE YOU BUILDING THIS EVENT AROUND AND WHY?

With this event, whom are we trying to reach? Which biblical purpose is the primary one to focus on? If we're going after unchurched students, we focus on evangelism. If we're taking a bunch of our kids on a mission trip, serving is the biggest priority. A discipleship retreat should look completely different than an outreach event.

79 GOAL: DEFINE WHAT SUCCESS MEANS FOR THE EVENT

How many students are we shooting for? Is it a fair number? Is it a faith number? There should also be more to a goal than just getting 50 students to an event. Look for ways to measure success in spiritual growth, participation, and meaningful conversations.

80 EXPLANATION: CLEAR UP CONFUSION

Can you define insider language? Are there terms or expressions used year after year that alienate new team members? This might be a good time for some basic questions.

81 SPECIFICS/BUDGET: PEOPLE AND MONEY MANAGEMENT

What are the next steps in pulling off the event? Assign jobs and key roles at this point in the meeting. This is the time to focus on the big picture of people management. How much are we spending on this event? Are there scholarships? Are we expecting to break even? What is the "magic number" for attendance?

82 VOLUNTEERS: WHO IS DOING WHAT?

Think through where you need people in the meeting area: registration, greeters, security patrolling the known make-out spots in the church. Remember that your volunteers around the table will be your best recruiters outside this room.

83 MARKETING: HOW TO LET STUDENTS KNOW ABOUT THE EVENT

One of the most critical tasks of a leader is marketing. The last thing you want to do is have an event for non-churched students and only your core kids show up. Make sure you are exploring the various channels for marketing, including text messaging, the church's website, an announcement in big church, or even skywriting.

84 FOLLOW-UP: WHERE WE DO GO FROM HERE?

When are we meeting again? When is the official debrief time? What time is the celebration party to honor what God has done?

Having covered these bases, you wrap up the meeting confident that your team is both inspired and informed. The countdown clock is running, but your team is set up to stay comfortably ahead of it and launch a great event. You might actually even get some sleep tonight.

2 TYPES OF CAMP TRAINING

As we were walking around the cabins last night, my friend and I were talking about how each of the respective leaders was doing exactly what we expected. Some were towing the line; others had a loose grip of control on their cabin. Some leaders were loud and crazy; others were quiet and reserved. Some let their kids get away with murder; others stopped pranks at the idea stage. And even though we had few problems at camp this year, as I looked at the situation, I thought we should potentially add a second layer to our camp training. Here's what we do right now and an idea for next year:

85 WHAT WE ALREADY DO– GENERAL TRAINING [GROUP]

We have a volunteer meeting before camp set-up the week before we leave. All of the counselors assemble together and we talk about the general expectations and the heart of the trip. We go over the camp schedule, talk about some of the quirks of the camp, and address specific rules that need to be highlighted before camp. It is a great chance for everyone to be in community, pray, and gear up for the big trip.

86 WHAT WE NEED TO ADD– SPECIFIC TRAINING [INDIVIDUAL]

We should take some time, in addition to the general training, to spend one-on-one time with each leader. We would look at what happened in previous years at camp (if applicable) and set this person up to win this year.

We could spend time beforehand thinking about the leader's personality and typical interaction with students, and we'd help guide that person in the specific areas of weakness. If we saw a potential weak spot, we would help guide the leader to a better place before something arises at camp.

Most camp counselors know how to run a work camp or ball game -- it is the personal issues that require the most coaching and guidance. So is this more work? It sure is. But it's worth it!

The People on the Bus Go Round and Round

Just a short time ago I officiated the memorial service for an 18-year-old student, one of the most challenging aspects of student ministry. This week, I was talking to a student whose mother passed away and not too long ago, he lost his father as well. He's just about to turn 17 and just became an orphan. We spent some time talking about his parents, the future and how he was handling it all. We talked about youth group, friends, Heaven and Jesus.

Later I was talking it all over with my wife. Her observation was that so much of what we do in youth ministry is about processes, vision-casting, pathways and teachings — creating this huge bus-like machine to help move students forward.

But sometimes the key is to just pull the bus over and care for the people who are along for the ride. It has to be a drop-everything-nothing-else-matters kind of moment that defines our ministry.

As you work on the bus — the machine of youth ministry — this week, make sure you take the time to minister to the people who are on board.

3 WAYS TO MAKE THE MOST OF YOUR DAY OFF

I enjoyed a rare weekend off — and spent some time this week thinking about principles that should guide my time off in the future. But before you read further — you do take a day off, right?

87 IT ONLY TAKES A SECOND TO BE PULLED BACK IN: TURN YOUR PHONE OFF

There's no shame in being completely offline for a day. You're playing with fire if you are always "on"— so make sure you turn off the electronic tether and set yourself free. Shut down Outlook™, unplug the Internet, forget "webmailing" for just a second, disable Twitter™, or have your spouse hide your phone. I am amazed how many times I instinctively look at my phone, only to be greeted by a blank screen because my wife turned it off.

88 HAVE A LIFE OUTSIDE OF THE OFFICE; FOCUS ON PEOPLE YOU LOVE

I love focusing on video games to relax on a day off. I love focusing on my hobby. I love focusing on my blog. I love writing and reading. But a great way to get the most out of your precious days off is to spend them focusing on the people you love. If you have kids, write up a family "bucket list" and do it with them. If you rarely see your spouse, get a sitter – start a babysitting ministry if you want to score some free ones – and go see a movie without the kids. People, people, people.

89 GOODNIGHT, SWEETHEART; CATCH UP ON SLEEP

Don't waste the whole day away in bed – but definitely carve out some time to sleep. With kids in school I can't exactly sleep in, but I can get to sleep earlier or try to squeeze in a nap. Pushing yourself hard during the work week is acceptable, even required at times, so make sure you balance it on the other end. Remember, sleep is not a sign of weakness.

4 REASONS WE DON'T TAKE TIME OFF

I'm not sure we would ever actually say these things out loud, but from time to time I catch myself thinking crazy thoughts that cause me to work harder and longer until I'm on the brink of burning myself out. I'm the hamster on that stupid wheel, and it has to stop! I'm sure I'm not the only one who plays this game in my head, right? Maybe you've said something like this before...

90 "IF I'M GONE THIS WEEKEND, IT WILL ALL FALL APART..."

A more arrogant thing has never been said. We're afraid it will all come crashing down when we're gone, so we do our best to maintain a sense of control each weekend by being present. Week to week we try to hold it all together to please the elders of the church and the unrealistic expectations we place on ourselves. Here's a groundbreaking theory: It won't fall apart while you're gone – and if it does, maybe that's exactly what needed to happen.

91 "PEOPLE WON'T UNDERSTAND IF I'M GONE FOR SERVICES..."

I've heard people actually say, "They already think that I only work one day a week – I can't afford the perception that I'm being lazy." Know this: You will be a better example to your students and to the parents in your ministry if you model a balanced family life that includes getting away for a few days every once in a while.

92 "I CAN'T GET AWAY – I'M ON CALL 24/7..."

There are times to break up a romantic dinner with your spouse. There are times when you need to drop everything and run to the hospital. Everything but the most extreme cases can wait until morning. Just make sure you jump into the crisis first thing when you get into the church office.

93 "I LOVE MINISTRY – I JUST CAN'T TEAR MYSELF AWAY!"

This is the big one for me; I really do love what I do. But I'm a firm believer that a little distance goes a long way in helping restore perspective and energize new directions. Let your love be renewed by spending time with friends that don't have anything to do with youth ministry. Refuse to talk about church. Tear yourself away at all costs.

Don't believe the lies that we as youth workers tell ourselves. Healthy youth ministry has a healthy youth minister – you probably need to take some time off. Turn off your phone. Unplug your computer. Throw your pager away – if you still have one, it's time to let it go anyhow. Drive to another state for a quiet BBQ dinner. Do whatever it takes to get away to be refreshed. Your future depends on it.

You know, I've really enjoyed the last few days off.

I took a trip to the Dominican Republic recently and when I got back I only spent a couple of hours in the office catching up. A weekend off in youth ministry is rare, so I know to appreciate it when it arrives. Here are a few recent thoughts about the dangers of always "being on" in youth ministry:

94 YOU'RE ONLY IN PROBLEM-SOLVING MODE

You're so busy solving other people's problems that you don't think about your own issues. When the pace of life increases, we tend to focus on helping others, and not ourselves. Every message is applied to someone else's situation; every learning is to be taught to another audience. One of the dangers of always being "on" is that until you turn it off you won't look deeply into your own life. I wonder sometimes if busyness and others-focused-to-a-fault is to protect the real me from coming to the surface.

95 YOU SACRIFICE THOSE THAT MATTER MOST

Always being on robs from those you would be with if you were off. And while taking your son with you to an event is one thing, taking your wife to summer camp doesn't count as a vacation. When you are always "on" as a pastor, you justify the need to do ministry at the expense of the people closest to you.

96 YOU HOLD THE MINISTRY TOO TIGHTLY

If you're always working, there's nothing left to lead and no decisions to be made. When you're gone or off, other people have to step up. Loosening the grip of leadership and control allows others to take responsibility. Let go and it will grow.

97 YOU BEGIN TO TAKE SHORTCUTS

In an effort to slow down the pace or at least pace yourself for the rest of the youth ministry "on" marathon, you only have two options -- well, three, if you count death as an option. 1) You can run faster. Dig deeper, work later, try harder, and get it all done. Or, 2) you can take shortcuts. It starts with the small things to help you save time, but eventually spirals into spiritual and character issues. When you run hard and don't stop, at some point you have to try and stop the pain, so you cut through no man's land and hope you don't get caught.

98 YOU WILL EVENTUALLY LEAVE YOUTH MINISTRY

Here's the endgame – if you don't quit every once in a while, you will eventually quit altogether. Youth ministry can be a tireless machine of good in the life of students. It can be a tireless machine that chews up good youth workers, too. I've been doing youth ministry long enough to see so many leave this calling/profession. There are a lot of good reasons to quit; being irresponsible with your time and always being "on" is certainly not one of them.

So you have my permission! Take some time OFF and get a break from always being ON. You'll be better off for it, I promise.

I ♡ SUMMER INTERNS

Summer interns are a total risk. Let's be honest — 72 days is barely enough time to start to figure a place out, much less really make a difference. So why go to all of that trouble? This attitude is why many people waste summer interns, relegating them to meaningless tasks that typically involve collation, stapling, getting coffee, or other assorted tasks any entry-level robot can do.

Here are reasons I love summer interns and you should, too:

99 SUMMER INTERNS GET THE VISION

Our summer internship is actually a closed program. If you want to get in, you must be a graduate from our ministry. We only take the cream-of-the-crop internal candidates – and that typically gives us students who really know and live out their faith, truly get the vision and direction of the ministry, and come in with a leg up over an outsider. They understand the culture, and while they still have no idea what they are getting into, they're more ready than you might expect.

Youth Ministry Fumbles

Fumble! Every player on the field scrambles in a mad dash for the ball. Nothing else matters at this very second except one thing: recover the ball now before the other team gets it.

But this time it is different. Instead of recovering the fumble, players immediately start to blame each other and point fingers at who goofed and argue about what just happened. It doesn't matter though, because the ball is sitting right there on the turf, waiting for someone to pick it up. Players choose to protect their interests and defend themselves over winning the game.

This happened to me last week at a big event we were pulling off. Here's what I learned, maybe it'll help you out next week: there will always be a dropped ball. At your next service, someone will throw a bad pass. There's no doubt that a volunteer or a team member will fumble this week. Hey, you might have given them a bad handoff, for that matter.

But pick up the ball. There's nothing more important in that moment.

Afterwards, review the film to see what happened and spend some time debriefing to make sure it doesn't happen again. Coach your players in how to react and respond to situations instinctively. My heart is that everyone on the team will pick up the ball and run with it.

100 SUMMER INTERNS HAVEN'T BEEN BROKEN YET

I like the greenness (is that even a word?) of a summer intern. They are eager to jump in; they want to prove themselves. They bring fresh eyes to a ministry that might consist of mundane and predictable programs. They say "yes" to things others might balk at – like the one time we had a summer intern wear a toga during the Olympic Games. Brilliant! Not being broken or jaded is a big deal.

101 SUMMER INTERNS ADD BANDWIDTH

I figure a typical summer intern will provide about 40% of what a paid staff member may contribute in the same workweek. You need to cut interns some slack because they are short-term and new, and because you want to pour into them while seeing results they produce. While I'm pleased to say that we are a "teaching student ministry," we also take full advantage of summer interns to help us get things done. The more hands, the merrier, I say. Let's get things done.

Having summer interns is not without challenges, but I couldn't be more excited about having the extra bandwidth for tasks and more heart as pastors to minister to our students.

4 RESPONSIBILITIES OF SUMMER INTERNS

I've been thinking about the importance of having a summer intern program where interns are challenged in their leadership ability, grow personally, and get a chance to openly serve and learn fundamental skills. Here's the arrangement I'm working on as we're about to dive in with summer interns joining the team:

102 YOU'LL GET TO LEAD A REAL PROJECT

We're going to look at what you bring to the table and let you own something big. It might be a series of events, it might be a particular big weekend, or it might be coordinating volunteers and staff around a signature event. You will not leave this summer without getting a chance to lead and try out some of the skills God has given you and you've been developing. Prepare to experience accountability from the environment and the team helping push you on to greatness.

103 YOU'LL GET TO PARTNER WITH AN ADULT LEADER ON SOMETHING SIGNIFICANT

Partnerships create a little less pressure than running the show, but your name is still on the line. This will give you a chance to work with a direct report "boss" and help pull off something big. You could be working on a script, a video, a series – and the deadline could be the Friday after you start or the Friday before the summer ends. Navigating interpersonal work relationships and responding are skills best learned in the forgiving role of an intern.

104 YOU'LL GET TO FUNCTION AS A TEAM PLAYER AND PITCH IN TO THE CULTURE OF OUR MINISTRY

This one is really the freedom to serve. Bring your specialty to the table, and bring your strengths over to combat a weakness. Perception and discernment will help you grow leaps and bounds this summer. Quickly analyze the situation and see how you can contribute to help the team reach its goals. The more you put in here, the more fulfillment and growth you will have, and the more partnerships and leadership will be granted.

105 YOU'LL GET TO WORK WITH STUDENTS ... AND ME!

I promise that we'll spend time together every other week over the summer. It will probably involve a Grand Slam Breakfast. I'll also make sure that you don't just work with adults and projects, but you get to spend some time with students. I know that a lot of youth ministry involves leading and caring for adults, but I also want you to touch, see, and feel the people God has called you to serve. I know your heart will get bigger this summer as a result.

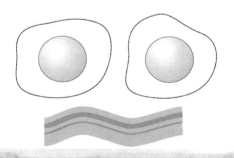

5 SKILLS YOUR NEXT YOUTH PASTOR MUST HAVE

If I were a senior pastor, this is what I would be looking for in a youth pastor. If I were a youth pastor, this is who I would be striving to become. Wait a minute, I am a youth pastor! Here are five skills I believe that youth workers must have:

106 HAS TO: WORK WELL WITH ADULTS

The job of the youth pastor is not really to work with students. You might have already figured that out – if not, you will someday soon. A youth pastor's primary role is to lead and care for the adult volunteer leaders, who can then minister to students. If you want to hire a great youth worker, it should be a person who is great with adults.

107 HAS TO: VALUE THE VISION OF THE CHURCH

Youth ministry too quickly slips into the temptation to go its own way. That isn't healthy, so when you hire a youth worker, remember that the person's belief in the direction and leadership of the church is something you cannot live without. Perhaps this is why many churches hire from within, because they have confidence they are getting someone who is totally on board. Youth workers have gotten a bad reputation from moving in directions that conflict with their church's leadership, so make sure your next hire is completely on board.

The Genealogy of Youth Ministry

"... Zerubbabel was the father of Abiud. Abiud was the father of Eliakim. Eliakim was the father of Azor. Azor was the father of Zadok. Zadok was the father of Akim. Akim was the father of Eliud. Eliud was the father of Eleazar. Eleazar was the father of Matthan. Matthan was the father of Jacob. Jacob was the father of Joseph, the husband of Mary. Mary gave birth to Jesus, who is called the Messiah." Matthew 1:13-16

I was given a new Bible recently from a friend of a friend, so I started reading right from the very beginning.

The New Testament opens with a survey of the genealogies from Abraham to Jesus, hardly the way to open a book as epic as the Bible, in my opinion? This guy had this son; this guy had this son, throw in a prostitute here or a king there. Boring. My mind wandered as I read the first chapter of Matthew. But there's a great message in there that hit me — these are the people that played their part in bringing Jesus to the world.

These men and women, some epic successes and some epic failures, were part of the line of Christ. I read over this list with new excitement after this realization: I am a part of this same line. So are you!

I get to join hundreds of people, some epic successes and some epic failures, in bringing Jesus to the world. My youth ministry team, your youth group, all followers of Christ even —all of us get to join in on this amazing genealogy. We're not part of the blood-line that brought about the birth of Jesus; we are part of the legacy of followers that bring spiritual rebirth of Jesus to the world.

Now I couldn't be more excited by the way that God opened up the New Testament. My youth ministry is part of the genealogy of Jesus Christ.

108 HAS TO: BE COMPLETELY FREE OF ARROGANCE OR PRIDE

Okay, this one isn't exactly possible, because we all stumble here. I would just say if someone has confidence or skills, I'm very interested. If a candidate feels the least bit arrogant or prideful, the answer is a quick and easy no. The heart of the youth worker, often overlooked in the wake of numerical success or electric charisma, is the ultimate key to successful ministry. If you sniff out something you don't like during any part of the hiring process, immediately move on to the next candidate.

109 HAS TO: BE A SERVANT

This one isn't too hard to sniff out, but search committees are too often drawn to flash and style over substance. Just because someone interviews well doesn't mean that person will serve your church well. A great gauge of a person's ministry heart can be seen in servanthood. Show me a servant, and I'll show you someone who gets it and someone I want as a model of faith to my students.

110 HAS TO: VALUE FAMILY

The person who gives everything to ministry and nothing to family isn't someone I want to hire. Listen to the way the candidate treats his or her children. Watch the interaction between the spouses. Pray for discernment that God will lead you to a person who cares about their own children as they do for the students in your church. Family must be a top priority.

Chances are, you won't be in the church you're currently serving at for the rest of your life. When God moves you on, here are the three things that I hope describe you on your way out:

111 **WORK** HARD TO STAY MENTALLY ENGAGED

It's like you are a high school senior in February – graduation is the only thing that matters, so good luck paying attention in class. One of the most challenging aspects of moving on is staying engaged. But while it is difficult, it is the right thing to do. Be on time to work, focus on the little things that demonstrate you're still caring and thinking about the ministry, fight off the "lame duck" pressure, and finish strong.

112 **WORK** HARD TO THE LAST DAY

You can ditch meetings that are solely future-oriented, but if there's something that involves you or would benefit from your involvement, be there! Overcome the temptation to detach yourself from the ministry. So get to work – even stay late if you need to! You reveal the depth of your character when you show up.

WORK HARD ON THE HANDOFF

The handoff to the next youth worker is typically the biggest fumble in most youth ministry leadership transitions. And while sometimes this just isn't possible, it would be a shame to let all of the hard work and progress over the last few years stall out or even move backwards. If there's no candidate for the position and no volunteer showing promise, at least consider making a handbook of timely information that can be handed off to the next leader. If there's an heir-apparent to the youth ministry, spend time working that person into the planning and operation of the youth ministry so he or she gets the feel for it.

Maybe you'll never have to leave – but if you do, finish strong!

NEXT

002

Thank You

Youth ministry can be a thankless job.

At the same time I would argue it can be one of the most compelling and fulfilling jobs in the world. But there's no doubt that often times we are under appreciated. In the craziness of church management, senior pastors can overlook a youth worker's effort. A friend outside of the church doesn't understand youth ministry entirely and the reckless abandon to do what you do. Students, whose lives have been changed as a result of the ministry, don't run up to you every weekend with a giant hug and tell you how much you are loved and appreciated.

Tonight I was mulling over the story of Jesus and the 10 Lepers (Luke 17:11-19). Jesus heals 10 men with leprosy, giving them a second shot at life. The men rush away, and sometime later, only one of them comes back to say thank you.

I think this is a great picture of youth ministry! Students have been healed and lives have been changed—but the "thank you ratio" is way off. I do love those moments when a former student comes back to the church after a few years of being away and shows appreciation. I love the emotion when a student's life is changed and they can't help but thank you. And I know that if I expect to be thanked, I'll usually be disappointed.

The most important thing to remember is that even if no one thanks you for doing what you are doing, you are healing people and setting them free. Embrace the ones that return to thank you, but remember those will be rare treasures. If Jesus only got one out of ten thank yous… then I'm in real trouble.

Thank you for serving in youth ministry. It is an honor to serve in the profession with you.

.com

More than Dodge Ball.com

A place set aside for words and pictures about this thing we call youth ministry.

Updated daily by Josh Griffin